G000112074

DAVID HOLLOWAY

Derby Day

Folio Miniatures

MICHAEL JOSEPH
LONDON

FOLIO MINIATURES

General Editor: John Letts

First published 1975 in Great Britain by
Michael Joseph Limited
52 Bedford Square London WC1B 3EF
in co-operation with The Folio Press

© *1975 David Holloway*

ISBN 0 7181 1303 9

PRINTED AND BOUND IN BELGIUM
by Henri Proost & Cie p.v.b.a., Turnhout

FORECAST

This short book is not intended to be a history of the Derby. It would be impertinent for me to try to write one when Roger Mortimer has compiled in *The History of the Derby Stakes* a superb volume describing every race from 1780 to 1973. Here the reader will find very few names of horses mentioned, or, for that matter, names of owners or riders. Nor is this an attempt to give a picture of *one* Derby Day in the way that Frith's painting is a portrait of a single occasion. What I have tried to do is to present Derby Day at its best and its worst on the basis of a whole lot of accounts, with glances backward and forward. Most of the material that I have drawn on was written in the 1850s and 1860s since this was the heyday of Derby Day as an institution and it is this that I am trying to celebrate.

David Holloway

SELECT BIBLIOGRAPHY

Anon. *Horse Racing: Its History*. Saunders Otley, 1863.

Charles Dickens. *The Old Curiosity Shop*. Oxford University Press, 1951.

Gordon Home. *Epsom*. Homeland Association, 1901.

Guy B. H. Logan. *The Classic Races of the English Turf*. Stanley Paul, 1901.

Roger Mortimer. *The History of the Derby Stakes*. Michael Joseph, 1973.

Eric Parker. *Highways & Byways in Surrey*. Macmillan, 1908.

Henry Pownall. *History of Epsom by an Inhabitant*. Dorling, 1825.

D. E. N. Southworth. *The Bride of an Evening*. Milner, n.d.

'Sylvanus'. *The Bye-lanes and Downs of England*. Bentley, 1859.

The author would like to thank the Reference Librarian of Epsom Public Library for access to the special collection of Derby books, newspaper cuttings and typescripts held at the Library.

The Derby Day from *Illustrated London News*, 1871
(The Mansell Collection)

DERBY DAY

'I need not say', said that great racing man Lord George Bentinck in the House of Commons on 23rd May, 1848, 'that tomorrow is Derby Day. As that is recognised as a holiday in the metropolis, I have obtained the sanction of the noble lord, the first minister of the Crown, to my motion.' For the second year running Lord George was proposing that the House of Commons should take Derby Day off. It was a strangely English way of doing things for, of course, Derby Day was not an official holiday, never had been and never would be, yet the members of the House of Commons wanted to join a large number of their constituents in observing it as one. Perhaps the Prime Minister of the day, Lord John Russell, put it better when he spoke in support of Bentinck's motion: 'As it seems the practice to look upon tomorrow as a national fête, I have acquiesced to the motion.' And so the motion was passed with only a few Scottish members (Scottish affairs were due for discussion that Thursday) voting against it.

'A national fête' was what Lord John called it; and by the 1840s that was what Derby Day had become and was to remain ever since. Some people even went so far as to call it a 'National Saturnalia', but if it was, it was a very restrained one. Four years before Lord George's speech in the House of Commons, the members of a Parliamentary Committee enquiring into the evils of gambling were asking their witnesses why the Derby was different. It was left to a Mr Barnard, described in an anonymous History of Horse Racing, published in 1863, as 'a gentleman of long experience in racing matters', to explain exactly why.

Here is part of his examination about Derby Day.

Q: Do not a great number of the lower classes go as a holiday, without joining in the gambling?
A: Yes, they do not join in the gambling; I should think they have no money to lose.

Q: Do not great numbers of the lower classes attend every year?

A: Yes.

Q: How many should you say of the lower classes?

A: Very like 15,000 or 20,000.

Q: Who do not gamble?

A: I should say not.

Q: The Derby day is a holiday for everyone?

A: Yes.

Q: Persons who work hard the whole of the rest of the year go to Epsom?

A: They make up their minds to go to Epsom.

Q: They are going down all the morning and coming back all the night?

A: Yes.

So that was it: everyone made up their minds to go to Epsom on Derby Day—and certainly not only the working classes. A sociologist of the time, had one existed, would have discovered that the workers were clearly outnumbered by the solid ranks of the middle and upper classes. But this was the National Fête where classes did not matter, least of all on the central rise, where carriages of all kinds were parked on the lower slopes, gypsies set up their booths at the top and all moved freely together. The real nobs might crowd into the Grand Stand and the other private stands ranged alongside it, but the true life was on the Hill. A forgotten Victorian novelist, D. E. N. Southworth, described the scene this way: 'It is the concentrated quintessence of the world with all its passions and objects, its hopes and fears, its loves and hatreds, its jealousies and rivalries, its joys and sorrows, its disappointments and triumphs.'

Before we look at the crowds, for the crowds are Derby Day, let us find out about their excuse for being there: the Derby Stakes—the 'Blue Riband of the Turf', as Disraeli called it. For most of the crowd the race is a confused jumble of horses and jockeys in the middle distance, a swirling mass of colour accompanied by the sounds of roaring crowds and of hooves thudding on grass. For the select few, who have the best vantage point, there is the chance of seeing the winner passing the post. Given a good start (and some years there were more than thirty false starts) the whole thing would be over in less than three minutes: 'Immortality for a horse in two minutes, forty-five seconds.'

No one quite knows when first there was racing on the rolling downs between Banstead and Epsom. Certainly there is evidence of horse races in Henry II's reign, but then any open, short-grassed area was suitable for a test of a horse's skill. The real story of the race begins in 1618 when one Henry Whicker first took his cattle to drink at a spring that he had found in a field at Epsom. The beasts refused to drink there and, when Whicker tasted it, he found the water decidedly unpleasant. The local apothecaries realised that he had discovered a mineral spring and, of course, by later refinement, Epsom salts. This was the nearest and most convenient medicinal spring to London and within twenty years the gluttons of the Stuart court were making the short journey to Epsom to take the waters to purge their livers and scour their intestines. Obviously they wanted entertainment while they took the cure and a whole collection of inns, gaming houses and cockpits grew up. What more natural than that the downland overlooking the town, as it was rapidly becoming, should be used as a racecourse? Soon there were races every day at noon, though it is questionable whether all of them were for horses. There were probably foot races and perhaps even coursing as well.

Horse-racing as a sport grew considerably during the early Stuart years. James VI and I and many of the Scots who came south with him were passionately fond of it. During the Civil War Charles I used the races at Epsom as an excuse to gather a group of cavalry together in order to attack various Parliamentary strongholds south-west of London though the ruse did not work and Charles's force was scattered. The popularity of the races and the waters at Epsom grew under Charles II and was described by Pepys, though he never seems to have been able to watch a race; public affairs had an unfortunate habit of intruding at the very moment when he was about to set off for Epsom.

7

William III and the first Georges took very little interest in horse-racing and none at all in Epsom which began to decline from favour—its springs had lost their potency, or appeared to have. A charlatan got hold of some local land and sank a well there but its contents, despite his claims, turned out to be totally unmedicinal.

Other watering places began to offer more genteel entertainment than that of the roistering Epsom scene and the town with its dancing places in the open air, its gambling houses and inns fell into decay. Annual horse races started again some time in the 1730s with heats in the morning and finals in the afternoon. Certainly by the middle of the century a Spring and an Autumn meeting were being held, but the pattern changed and the main Epsom meeting was moved from the Autumn to the week immediately preceding Whitsun, roughly where it remains today.

Epsom might well have remained just another small meeting had it not been that the twenty-one-year-old future Earl of Derby had taken the lease of a nearby converted alehouse, called the Oaks, which had been refurbished as a country house by his uncle by marriage, the General Burgoyne who surrendered to the American troops at Saratoga. Three years later the young man succeeded his grandfather as Earl. From his father, who had died just too soon to inherit the title himself, the young Earl inherited a love of horse-racing, but his real passion was for cockfighting. (It was perhaps his influence that persuaded the first promoters of the Derby to have cockfights as an additional attraction on race days in the early years.) In 1779 the Earl allowed the name of his house to be given to one of the Epsom races, the Oaks Stakes. Most races at this time were over long distances, anything up to four miles, but shorter distances were beginning to find favour and the promoters of the Oaks decided on a race of one mile for three-year-old fillies.

The idea was a success and the following year Lord Derby and his friends decided that there should be a similar mile race for all three-year-olds, and the Derby Stakes were instituted. There is, by the way, no truth in the old story that Lord Derby and Sir Charles Bunbury tossed up for the honour of giving their name to the race; Derby was always the prime mover. But Sir Charles had the satisfaction of owning the first winner, Diomed, and he picked up winnings of 1,075 guineas. Sir Charles (1740–1821) was in fact a far more important figure of the turf than Lord Derby. He was regarded as the Perpetual President of the Jockey Club and did much to build up the prestige of that body. There is no memorial to his name at Epsom but one exists at the headquarters of racing, Newmarket, where part of the course is known as the Bunbury Mile.

In the first year there were nine runners, the survivors of the thirty-six who entered, lining up to run the last mile of the old four-mile course used since the 1730s. This route sent the horses on a gallop round a fairly gentle right-hand curve to the one stable point of the Epsom course, the finishing post, the same today as that by which Diomed led home the first Derby field. (It was then such an unimportant race that no one knows now by what distance he won, certainly it was not worth reporting in a newspaper.) Four years later a new course was marked out, this time curving left-handed round the Hill towards Tattenham Corner and then joining the old straight for the last couple of furlongs. At the same time, the promoters decided that the distance should be raised to a mile and a half. Sixty years later, the start was brought closer to the Hill so that the deadly sharp downhill curve ending with Tattenham Corner should be made a shade more gentle. In 1872 the position of the start was altered by a few yards to the position it is in today and the course has remained the same except for a tiny adjustment to the alignment of Tattenham Corner.

By the 1790s, after an inauspicious beginning, the Derby was becoming popular. Not only was Epsom handy from London but the horse-racing men began also to realise what a supreme test of three-year-olds this undulating course could be. All the colts carried the same weight (the actual amount changed several times), allowance was made for fillies only, and the course, by accident rather than by design, was able to prove the qualities of a really tough horse. The character of the course has changed little since 1784. For the first half mile the ground is slightly uphill and then levels out until the left-hand turn where the course descends sharply (it is supposed to be the steepest hill on any English race course, other than the one at Brighton), rounds Tattenham Corner and then into the fairly short straight which rises gently to the finishing post. It is this last uphill section which often proves too much for the less able horses.

Crossing the Wandle from Panorama of the Road on the Derby Day, *Pictorial Times,* **1845 (The Mansell Collection)**

People come to see the Derby not because it is a better race than any other (there are certainly others as good). It is the situation of the Epsom course, only just over seventeen miles from the centre of London, that gives it its attraction, and the fact that the rolling nature of the country and the convenient way in which the course winds round in a flattened horseshoe form make it possible for a very large number of people to see at least something of the race, and at one time for nothing. And in those days, those who wished could patronise the stands with their private boxes and their view of the whole course; the fanatics could arrive early and take their place at their chosen point on the rails for a close-up view of at least a moment or two of the race. And for those who came for the Occasion, there was the Hill, the excitement of the masses of people there: the sight, over the heads of those who crowded the rails, of the jockeys' silks and even an occasional view of the head of a horse.

By and large, the people on the Hill were Londoners,

Crossing the Wandle from Panorama of the Road on the Derby Day, *Pictorial Times,* **1845 (The Mansell Collection)**

though some came from much further afield. So although the rich might stay with friends in the neighbourhood or put up at an inn for race week, and the gypsies and their kind might set up camp for the week on the Hill, for the majority the Derby was a day trip. Before the railway came to Epsom in 1848, the only way to come from London was by the turnpike road that wound its way through Clapham and Mitcham. On ordinary days the coaches that left London, particularly if driven by 'Little Robert', reputed to be 'the fastest whip on the road', would be pulling up at the Spread Eagle Inn in Epsom High Street in little more than two hours. (Robert Whittle took the 8 a.m. coach to London and brought it back at 5 p.m. the same evening). But on Derby Day, it was a very different story.

The roads were crowded with every sort of vehicle that could be pulled by horse or donkey—smart four-in-hand coaches whose posthorns and drivers cursed at the coster-mongers in their carts, overloaded broughams, wagonettes, barouches and even delivery vans. The narrow road was packed and there were long queues at the turnpike houses as drivers paid their dues. For those on the route who were left behind, this cavalcade formed the sight of the day as from dawn onwards the procession made its slow way past. Some of the travellers never made it. Seventeen miles was a long way for a horse that was probably accustomed to pulling a smaller load round the city streets and sometimes axles or harness broke beyond repair. And there were temptations by the way. Every tavern on the road had its doors wide open. On dry days the dust was appalling and parched throats needed drink. And on wet days to those suffering the cold discomfort of the long journey the idea of a glass of punch or gin made every inn seem tempting.

Some of the rogues who gathered for the Derby did not even bother to go as far as the course; there were plenty of pickpockets and tricksters to be found on the Epsom road and the more gullible might be persuaded to spend their all even before they reached journey's end. Even the tipsters operated at every wayside inn.

The nearer the course they got the thicker the crowds became. The dust clouds rose higher, white now from the chalk of the Downs. The entertainers, perhaps the ones who had arrived too late or did not feel strong enough to stand the competition of the Hill, set up their coconut shies and other attractions by the side of the road, and tumblers and acrobats put on their endless performances, begging the odd penny from the slow-moving convoy. Through the centre of Epsom the cavalcade wound its way then breasted the climb to the course. Just as the final straight sorts out the weaker horses, so this last hill took its toll of the weary beasts who had made the long haul from London. A fine demonstration of horsemanship, carriages swinging up the slopes of the Hill in style with horns blowing, was always greeted by applause. Or, transport abandoned by the road-side, the less fortunate finished the long, tiresome, jostling march with the rest of the foot travellers. For the lucky ones who arrived safely, there was the final struggle for a good vantage point.

Four railway stations stood at different places near the course. Those who came down on the race specials, usually trains made up of dirty carriages packed to overflowing, faced either the longish walk from the town, or else the battle for a cab, worming their way towards the drivers who yelled 'a bob a nob to the course!' Waving their whips the cabbies fought into the line of other vehicles making their way up the hill. Every inn would be overflowing with people needing to fortify themselves before they attempted the last part of the journey. Inching their way up to the course the whole colourful picture suddenly opened out before them all.

Was it the familiar scene of Frith's 'Derby Day', first exhibited in 1858, that they saw? Yes, but his picture was only a tiny bit of it. Multiply Frith's canvas a hundred times and you have some sort of picture of the Hill, the fair on the skyline whose booths, shies, roundabouts, gambling pits grew more elaborate as the years passed. Here was a great oriental market on a Surrey hilltop. At no other place was there ever such a gathering. The more formal atmosphere of Ascot did not provide the same happy hunting ground though many of those who operated on the Hill would move there later in the summer, and this was the one place where every fair merchant tried his luck. Lower down the hill the tipsters operated, shouting that they alone knew the winner or slyly whispering exclusive information from the stables. Also winding their way in and out of the parked carriages and carts were the salesmen and the performers who needed no fixed base—the acrobats, the wandering minstrels, those who sold their wares from trays, and the operators of illegal gambling games who needed to make a tricky get-away through the throng should a policeman come into sight.

The *Illustrated London News* of 23rd May, 1863, thus described the inhabitants of the great camp on the top of the hill: 'And here a more curious generation than these camp followers it would be difficult to find. They form a genus apart: a congerie of nomadic tribes, real Arabs of the desert, whose business it is to attend race courses and, by hook or by crook, scramble for a livelihood. They are passing honest; that is to say, if they can get their living honestly, and they have no direct incentive or irresistible temptation to dishonesty, they will refrain from picking and stealing ... It would be perhaps unkind to call them rogues and vagabonds, tramps and vagrants, beggars and cadgers. Let us employ the discreet phrase from Shakespeare's *Timon of Athens:* they are men "who much do need".'

The people of the Hill offered almost anything portable for sale that anyone would buy, including things that you would rarely see elsewhere like strange constructions out of brass wire, and sticky drinks and sweets of all sorts. They would operate endless games of chance more subtle and various than their modern successor, the mindless one-armed bandit. Everywhere there was noise—the shouts of the touts, the tipsters and the spielers outside the booths, whose owners wore silk waistcoats and hats with plumes. Outside the gambling pits stood servants in gorgeous liveries, soft-spoken and insinuating, wheedling the suckers in with promises of riches. Other men in country dress pretending to be simpletons volunteered to take part in games of chance. Their success would encourage the real suckers to take part, lose and keep losing.

And there was music everywhere, creating eternal discords as a hundred melodies—some of them sweet enough in themselves—blended impossibly in the general row. Some of the performers were gypsy fiddlers, others trained but unemployed musicians, who played every conceivable instrument with different degrees of skill. As the century went on the predominant musical figure was the Nigger Minstrel, with banjo, tambourine, concertina and bones. In the early morning his face, all except for his white-painted eyes and mouth, was shining black with burnt cork, but as the day wore on it would become parti-coloured as the sweat or, in bad weather, the rain made streaks down his make-up. His once white shirts and the bright waistcoats grew greyer and greasier.

There were formal boxing booths with crews of fighters at the top of the Hill but old prize fighters with flattened noses and battered faces needed only a bit of space to put on a performance which at least gave the impression of being in earnest, but however final the seeming knock-out at the end of it might be it was one that could be repeated quite easily a few minutes later in a different part of the crowd. Space, of course, was at a premium and trickery was needed to win it. One old gag was the use of a stooge who having carefully sucked a sliver of soap concealed in his mouth would fall down and thrash around foaming copiously at the mouth. As the crowd drew back obediently in answer to the cry, 'Give him air', two boxers would appear in the space which formed, slip on the gloves and go into their routine. The invalid, miraculously cured, would disappear into the crowd to wait for his share of the collection which would be taken at the end of the bout. Conjurers, too, performed their endless tricks and wherever anyone would listen ventriloquists argued with their dummies. It was a whole music hall of the open air.

On all sides there were ragged children, seemingly thousands of them, some (though few) true gypsies among them. Many were expert beggars, pickpockets and scroungers; while others tried their luck by turning a few inexpert cartwheels or offering rather pathetic bunches of flowers, gathered in lanes or filched from the gardens of nearby houses. Little Nell was one of these latter, and Dickens describes her in one of the short narratives so characteristic of him which bring a whole scene to life better than anyone else. (Dickens does not specify that the racecourse he is describing in *The Old Curiosity Shop* is Epsom, but he was a regular attender there and the whole scene fits Derby Day better than any other occasion.) Nell is walking in the crowd:

'The child bore upon her arm the little basket with her flowers, and sometimes stopped, with timid and modest looks to offer them at some gay carriage; but alas! there were many bolder beggars there, gipsies who promised husbands, and other adepts in their trade, and although some ladies smiled gently as they shook their head, and others

cried to the gentlemen beside them, 'See what a pretty face!'
they let the pretty face pass on, and never thought that it
looked tired and hungry.

There was but one lady who seemed to understand the
child, and she was the one who sat alone in a handsome
carriage, while two young men in dashing clothes, who
had just dismounted from it, talked and laughed loudly at
a little distance, appearing to forget her quite. There were
many ladies all around, but they turned their backs, or
looked the other way, or at the two young men (not un-
favourably at *them*) and left her to herself. She motioned
away a gipsy-woman, urgent to tell her fortune, saying it
was been told already, and had been for some years, but
called the child towards her, and taking her flowers put
money in her trembling hand, and bade her go home and
keep at home for God's sake.'

But, as I have already pointed out, the crowd did not
consist exclusively of fashionable middle-class people. A
mid-nineteenth century issue of the *Illustrated London
News* observed: 'On Derby Day the patrician puts his pride
into the pocket of his gossamer paletot and is perfectly
ready to be hail fellow well met with the humblest of the
working classes. None save the most ill-conditioned cur-
mudgeons lose their temper at the witticisms levelled at them
on the Hill or in coming and going. If things are thrown
at you, just throw them back. But there are limits—oranges
and lobster claws are just all right but not bags of flour or
bad eggs.'

In the early 1800s when Derby Day had not become a
great public occasion and the crowd was almost entirely
made up of racecourse roughs, the mood tended to be quite
ugly and, if things did not go to their liking, it could lay
on a considerable riot. But this sort of extreme rowdiness
(with flour and eggs) was the exception rather than the rule.
By the late 1840s all Victorian writers remark on the good
nature and the well-behaved character of the crowds.

The use of lobster claws and orange peel as ammunition
must have been tempting; this was no time or place for a
quick sandwich and a drink out of a thermos flask which

serve for a modern picnic. Those Victorians, for whom part of the most important business of the Derby, as one journalist described it, was 'to eat, drink and stare at one's neighbours', brought with them luncheon baskets of quite astonishing proportions complete with china, silver, white linen and wine glasses. Lobster salad was essential for the best picnic tables, but so were cold mutton, chickens, ducks, guinea fowls and huge game pies. You ate your fill, and washed it down with champagne and hock, presumably rather warm. As you worked your way through this pile of food, the beggars stared and waited for crumbs.

There was also a rather different sort of beggar, the hard-up young man who put on his best clothes and got to Epsom the best way he could, either by cadging a lift or going Third Class by train and walking to the course. Then he would quarter the Hill until he spotted someone with whom, timing it carefully, he could claim some slight acquaintance; and of course it would be thoroughly bad manners on the picnickers' part not to invite this hovering newcomer to join in their feast.

For those who did not bring their own drink and wanted something stronger than the ginger beer carried by the wandering pedlars there was the drink tent, famous for its bottled beer, which was much rarer in mid-Victorian times than it is today. Those who patronised the Grand Stand were not going to be denied their food either, particularly those on the upper decks who could only reach their vantage point by a very steep staircase.

Dickens, who was normally a visitor to the Hill, and not above scrounging food on occasions, went early one year to see the advance preparations being made in the Grand Stand, the huge structure more then 126 feet long, built to accommodate five thousand people, more than half of whom occupied the immense lead roof. He gave his impressions to the readers of *Household Words* (7th June, 1851):

'Here we are! Let us go into the basement. First into the weighing house, where the jockeys "come to scale" after each race. We then inspect the offices of the Clerk of the Course himself; wine-cellars, beer-cellars, larders, sculleries and kitchens, all gigantic, and as copiously appointed as if they formed part of an Ogre's castle. To furnish the refreshment saloon, the Grand Stand has in store two thousand four hundred tumblers, one thousand two hundred wine glasses, three thousand plates and dishes, and several of the most elegant vases we have seen outside of the Glass Palace, decorated with artificial flowers. An exciting odour of cookery meets us in our descent. Rows of spits are turning rows of joints before blazing walls of fire. Cooks are trussing fowls; confectioners are making jellies; kitchen-maids are plucking pigeons; huge crates of boiled tongues are being garnished on dishes. One hundred and thirty legs of lamb; sixty-five saddles of lamb; in short, a whole flock of sixty-five lambs have to be roasted and dished and garnished for Derby Day. Twenty rounds of beef, four hundred lobsters, one hundred and fifty tongues, twenty fillets of veal, one hundred sirloins of beef, five hundred spring chickens, three hundred and fifty pigeon pies; a countless number of quartern loaves, and an incredible quantity of ham have to be cut up for sandwiches; eight hundred eggs have got to be boiled for the pigeon pies and salads. The forests of lettuces, the acres of cress, and beds of radishes, which will have to be chopped up; the gallons of 'dressing' that will have to be poured out and converted into salads for the insatiable Derby Day, will be best understood by a memorandum from the chief of that department to the *chef-de-cuisine,* which happened, incidentally, to fall under our notice: "Pray don't forget a large tub and a birch broom for mixing the salad".'

Someone who might have witnessed those preparations with Dickens was Isabella Mayson, the fifteen-year-old step-daughter of the Clerk of the Course, the eldest of a double family of twenty-one children. Just over ten years later she was to compile the most famous cookery book of all time, *Mrs Beeton's Book of Household Management.*

The Grand Stand was seven years older than she was. By the late 1820s the race had become so popular that the erection of a huge stand for use in only two meetings a year was still thought to be a good business proposition. To build it, £20,000 was raised with no trouble at all in one thousand £20 shares, and the actual structure was put up for £13,890. A feature of the stand was its tiers of boxes which were necessary because there was no equivalent to the Ascot lawn and ladies who were not admitted to the betting ring or the club enclosures could only take exercise by perambulating from box to box. Other stands were put up on either side. Curiously enough the Grand Stand was not

The New Royal Stand at Epsom from *Illustrated London News,*
1875 (Mary Evans Picture Library)

directly in line with the finish and was three hundred yards away from the paddock, so those who wished to see the horses walking in the ring being saddled and mounted, had to hurry back along the course in order to be in their seats in time for the parade. The distance was so great that in fact the Prince Consort rode down to see the saddling on the occasion when he visited the Derby with Queen Victoria in 1840.

There had always been a royal connection with the race: the Duke of Cumberland's Eclipse was an also ran in the very first Derby and in 1788 the Prince of Wales (later

George IV) won the race with the favourite, Sir Thomas. A few years later the Prince was involved in a scandal involving the running of one of his horses at Newmarket and he forswore racing for a time. Later he took it up again but never with the same interest. William IV had a Derby runner but it was not placed in the 1831 race; he was not interested in racing of any sort and certainly made no point of attending the Derby. The great moment designed to give the Derby the royal seal of approval should have come in 1840 when Queen Victoria came to the Derby with Prince Albert. She arrived, not by the public road, but by way of a private park; these were the hungry forties when people were restive and not all that fond of royalty, and her reception was not generous. There certainly were crowds around the royal carriage but some of the shouted remarks were less than loyal. The Queen was not amused and decided rapidly that the Derby was not to her taste.

But it was very much to the taste of her eldest son when, twenty-three years later, he paid his first visit to the Derby. This time royalty was welcomed with enthusiasm. He became a regular attender and a successful owner. When his horse Persimmon won the Derby in 1896 there was tremendous excitement on the course. Roger Mortimer describes it in his *History of the Derby Stakes* (Michael Joseph, London, 1973): 'As Persimmon walked back towards the unsaddling enclosure, the Downs echoed from one end to another with the cheers that were renewed again and again. Even the most dignified individuals in the stands for once let themselves go, and it was a truly remarkable exhibition of spontaneous enthusiasm and delight. The only glum face on the course was that of Watts (the Prince's jockey) who had been having a great deal of trouble with his weight. Wasting always brought on fits of depression, which he tried to relieve, according to Marsh (the royal trainer), "by indulging in an occasional stimulant." However Watts at length permitted himself the luxury of a smile when Marsh, who had fought like a rugby forward to get to his horse, slapped him on the thigh and shouted, 'Don't you realise you've just won the Derby for the Prince of Wales?' The cheering reached its peak as the Prince came forward to lead his horse in, and all in all it was a scene that could never be forgotten by those who saw it.'

Six years later the Prince of Wales won the Derby again with Diamond Jubilee but this was nothing compared with the occasion when in 1909 he became the first reigning monarch to win the Derby. Minoru flashed past the post in two minutes forty-two and three-fifths seconds, just a short head in front of Louviers with William the Fourth only half a length away, third. As the news came through that Minoru had indeed won—there were no photo finishes then and the order depended entirely on the eye of the judge to decide which of the three horses had passed the post first—the entire crowd burst into the National Anthem led by a famous music hall singer, the sound growing and swelling as the singing, started by those round the King, spread across the course and right up the Hill. No other reigning monarch has won the Derby but King George VI came close to it with Big Game in 1942, a hot favourite who faded in the straight. It has, however, for many years been the custom for the royal family to watch the Derby. There is not the formality of Royal Ascot, no house party going day after day to the races. The monarch joins her people on a day trip.

The rather smug witness I have quoted who gave evidence to the Parliamentary Committee that the lower classes did not bet was only speaking part of the truth. Some did not bet but a great many more did. What makes the Derby different from any race other than the Grand National is that people who have never been to a race meeting and would not dream of betting on other occasions did so and do. Today, of course, there are betting shops almost everywhere, and shortly before them most milkmen did a thriving trade in carrying housewives' bets to street bookmakers on Derby Day. In Victorian times, the ladies such as those who grace Frith's canvas would not have been allowed anywhere near a bookie, and very few of them would have known their milkman, even if they had one. (Most urban milk was carried around by strong girls with great pails hanging from yokes over their shoulders.) By a curious convention the ladies of the latter half of Victoria's reign usually bet with pairs of gloves as currency. I suppose that since they wore gloves of one sort or another most of the time, they must have gone through a great many pairs in a year, and if the bet were with a man there could be no embarrassment for either of them in paying off a bet in this currency. The odds paid on gloves, by the way, reflected the cash odds offered by the bookmakers.

In the early days of the Derby most money changed hands through private wagers, usually made between the owners and their friends. These bets could be huge. A conversation is reported between Lord George Bentinck and Lord Glasgow: 'Does anyone', asked Lord George, 'wish to lay three to one against my horse?' When Lord Glasgow volunteered, Lord George added: 'Very good, but I don't want any small bets.' Lord Glasgow replied: 'Nor I; if ninety thousand to thirty will suit you, I will buy it.' Even so great a gambler as Lord George took fright at this. (He was wise; his horse lost that year.)

With the population largely illiterate, bookmaking was a difficult trade but by the 1820s and 1830s professional bookies were starting to make their appearance, and a pretty villainous crew they were. Yet in a sense they were only reflecting the morals of others in the racing world. More or less anything went. Bookies might try to nobble a horse—not with any subtlety or secret drugs but quite simply by laming it or poisoning it. In 1844 an owner nearly succeeded in winning the race with a four-year-old. (Mr A. Wood's Running Rein, first past the post, was later proved to be a four-year-old called Maccabeus running in disguise.) Jockeys were open to bribes to throw a race—there were not a few surprising Derby losers—and trainers were suspect as well. So it was only natural that bookmakers were villains too—certainly they were treated as such. In the days before the Grand Stand was built and even for a time afterwards the bookies were kept at a distance. They formed their ring at the crest of one of the Downs round the remaining stump of an old gibbet. 'Sylvanus', the author of *Bye-lanes and Downs of England* describes the scene at an early Derby

22

and gives a strange picture of the sort of people who might be seen in the ring: 'The ponderous prelate and his ponderous Grace; my Lord George, the bold baker, and Mr Unwell; Sir Xenophon Sunflower, the Assassin, and the flash grazier; the Dollar, hellite, billiard-marker and bacon-factor; the ringletted O'Bluster, the double-jointed publican, Leather Lungs and Handsome Jack, contrasted in pig's skin; and, ye Centaurs! what seats were there!'

'Sylvanus' describes the scene as they ride up to the ring:

'At the time we write of, "Old Crutch", with his scaffolding under his arm, and disabled limb dangling like a loose girth from his rosinante's side—a quadruped equalling the Dollar's mount in beauty—might have been seen side by side with Lord Chesterfield, on his thoroughbred, and addressing him in all the Timbobbinish horrors of his frightful vernacular. My lord was then in the zenith of his good humour, and was, moreover, so well upon Cotherstone, that he saw graces in Old Crutch's physog, with the charming "thousand to forty" he hoped to draw from him of on the Tuesday *prochain*—that he joked and rattled with the uncouth old cripple in undisguised merriment. With these might have been noticed the elegant form of Lord Wilton, on his roan, shaded again by a round-shouldered knave from Manchester, with ungloved hands and snub nose, who "potted the crack" for his special line of action. His yeoman Grace of Limbs, fresh and hearty as a summer gale, mounted on his Blue-eyed Maid, loomed in stalwart manhood by the side of some pallid greek or city trader, having a word of greeting and jollity for all alike, for *he* was there for the sake of the sport, and had no anxiety beyond his "pony".'

Later things became a trifle more organised, the bookies did not operate from horseback and the punters came on foot. But the noise was as tremendous as ever as the odds were called. As the clothes of the Victorian punters grew more sober in style, the bookies could still be seen with feathers in their hats and belts of silver coins round their waists. When they could write they put up phonetic versions of the horses' names on their boards with the odds, which they could calculate like a flash in their heads, written against them. In the ring were the big men, people like 'Crutch' Robinson, the one-legged man 'Sylvanus' was writing about, and beside him, among others, were a villainous pair of brothers, the Blands. As a rule the bigger the bookmaker, the less noise he made. It would have been difficult for them to 'welsh', they were too well known. But on the edge of the circle there were more shifty figures, not dealing with the rich punters but with the shillings and coppers of the small men. On a good day they would pay up, but should the favourite come romping home, they would leg it for theirs, for they had not the capital to carry them over such a disaster.

The bets on, the horses saddled and cantering down to the start, the crowd would settle down and even the steam engines of the roundabouts at the top of the Hill would grind to a halt. Then the long wait: with a big field, and from the 1840s and 1850s onwards there were usually more than twenty runners, sometimes over thirty, it took time to have the roll called, the girths tightened. Before starting gates there would be any number of false starts. A great deal of gamesmanship among the jockeys was involved, sometimes those from the north and south ganged up on each other. Then finally the flag was down and they were away, accompanied by the roars of those who could see and give some guidance to those who could not, the special time for pickpockets as necks were craned and attentions held. In less than three minutes it was all over. Before the telegraph and telephone lines came, confirmation of the race result was signalled by a flight of pigeons circling up and taking the news of the winner to newspapers and bookies in different parts of the country.

Those who had been lucky now rushed to the bookies to make sure that their man had not escaped; for the rest mutual commiserations, another drink, and maybe a visit to a gambling booth to try to win back the lost stake. There would be more races to watch, of course, but with the Derby over only in an atmosphere of anti-climax with the certainty of a long drive home up the jammed roads or the slow queue for the railway stations from which packed trains pulled their weary loads back to the city. Even the brightest day would seem a little duller now. The sense of camaraderie that had been so strong—Dukes and dustmen together—was no longer so obvious. As horse-drawn vehicles of all kinds moved down the Hill, what had been banter became more

**Tattenham Corner from an engraving by Gustave Doré
c. 1870 (The Mansell Collection)**

edgy as the slower carts got in the way of the four-in-hand coaches. The horns that had been blowing in cheerful salute now sounded in insult or warning.

As the London crowd, by far the largest contingent, made its way down to the Thames bridges, the light would be going. It would have been a long day. For the people of the Hill there would be the takings to count. Some would stay

25

the remaining two days of the meeting, but the pickpockets, the beggars, the real rogues would slide quickly away. For the poorest or the most rapacious, there was still the litter to go through: the left-overs already picked over by crews of gypsy dogs, the dropped money, the occasional ear-ring, the lost glove. Those who were staying would climb into their tents, their caravans, their booths or would just lie under blankets by the fires made of heaped-up litter. When the meeting was all over, they would be on the road again to the next races, the country fairs or the seaside, wherever there was a reasonably honest or moderately dishonest penny to be earned. For everyone tomorrow would be another day. The clerk and the costermonger who had stood side by side with the stockbroker and his wife on the Hill would be back in their places in the morning minus a day's pay and, if the wrong horse had won, maybe a great deal more.

Times change, but the Derby does not change so much. Coaches and carts give way to open-topped buses and charabancs, which since the demise of the coach and four are themselves called coaches. The noise became lessened in the genteel atmosphere of the late Victorian times when the strident sound of the steam organs was objected to, and in a society in which there were less rigid class lines, the camaraderie of the Hill gradually dwindled. Advertising began to make its way on to the Downs, with its hoardings and then for an astonishing while its kites, which given enough wind, would hover over the Hill on long strings, the bodywork proclaiming the virtues of soap, mustard or pills. Between the wars the aeroplanes made their appearance towing their long banners and sometimes even writing their advertising message in smoke in the sky.

All this, perhaps everything that I have written so far, implies blue skies. In an early English summer could the skies ever always be blue? Hardly. It even snowed on Derby Day in 1839 and 1867. On the second of these occasions, there was more than just a slight flurry of snow; there were heavy showers before and after the race. More often, though, there was just rain, anything from a slight drizzle to a

26

torrential thunder storm. True, if it was raining, there was no dust on the road, but the last part of the journey up to the course was made through mud the colour of dirty milk, and only the most sure-footed horse would be able to pull its load up to a decent point of vantage.

In his magazine, *All the Year Round*, Charles Dickens described what he called 'The Dirty Derby' of 1863 (inciden-

Derby Day from an engraving by Gustave Doré *c.* 1870
(The Mansell Collection)

tally it was the first one that Edward VII, then Prince of Wales, saw). The author had met an Irish friend who wanted to see the race, so early on a very wet morning they set out for Victoria Station from Dickens's home near Regents Park. At the station there were plenty of people but very little

27

excitement. 'We took tickets', Dickens recorded, 'for a damp little train just as if we were going to Birmingham'. A few sharp words followed with a showily dressed woman who tried to bring her fat husband into an already crowded railway carriage, and then they set off to arrive just half an hour later at a little damp rickety station, 'an oasis of boards in an ocean of mud.' Sliding down the road from the station they came to the centre of Epsom where, while drinking a reviving glass of brandy at the Spread Eagle Hotel, they watched the procession of carriages going by. Everyone was soaked to the skin. As Dickens and his companion made their way up the hill on foot towards the course, the mud got steadily worse until near the top it was a foot deep. The slow procession of mud-paddlers plodded on to reach the firm ground at the top where they were surrounded by small boys clutching handfuls of straws that they had pulled from the local haystacks with which they offered to clean the boots of the passers-by.

'Just as we reached the Grand Stand', Dickens continued, 'a rather shabby carriage dashed up to the door, and a howl of damp welcome announced that youthful royalty had arrived. Youthful royalty, presently emerging in a macintosh coat with a cigar in his mouth proved so attractive that any more progress in its immediate vicinity was impossible.' There poor Dickens and his friend found themselves completely hemmed in, 'jammed in a crowd the components of which were lower, worse, and wickeder than I have ever seen'. Among them he noticed prize fighters in dirty jerseys and seedy touts, 'thin, wiry, sharp-eyed little men with eyes strained and bleary from constant secret watching of racers' gallops.' There were also dirty, battered tramps and the sellers of cigar lights (they must have been pretty damp in this weather) and people offering unofficial and probably inaccurate race cards. And there were pickpockets, 'shifty and disgraceful, with no hope of a harvest in these surroundings', and there behind the Grand Stand were the Welshers, the small bookies, 'a parody of Tattersalls, poor pitiful varlets in greasy caps and tattered coats ... bellowing in hoarse ragged tones: "I'll bet against the field". Nobody seemed to take their bets.'

Eventually the press eased and Dickens was able to make his way slowly forward and across the course to the concourse on the Hill. 'We worked our way through the line of carriages, received a dozen invitations to lunch. We accepted a glass or two of sherry and then settled down to the

'Making the Favorite safe for The Derby' from an engraving by George Cruickshank c. 1850
(The Mansell Collection)

Derby.' They might have been damp and a bit disgruntled but at least they were there, and they did not seem to mind so much that the rain went on teeming down. One thing was evident, that the rain had deterred many of the people

29

who usually crowded the Hill and they had a better view than expected and could watch the police trying to clear the laggards from the course after the bell had rung. The last to leave was the inevitable dog, running a solo race. It is typical of the fact that Derby Day is an Occasion rather than just a race that Dickens did not bother to record who had won, or even that it was a most exciting sight. (The winner was Macaroni who came in a short head in front of the favourite Lord Clifden.) Perhaps Dickens had lost interest: that year there were thirty-four false starts. Anyway he plodded back to the station with the thought that 'last year it was iced champagne, claret cup and silk overcoats; now it ought to be hot brandy and water, foot baths and flannels.'

Even the dirtiest weather could not alter the occasion. At first even war could not do so, but news of the result was sent through by wire to those fighting in the Crimea. In 1914, Epsom was taken over for military use but the race did not die; it was transferred to Newmarket. This transfer happened again during the Second World War and there were always some thousand people with time off from their other duties to see the race on the Newmarket July course, though this was acknowledged to be a less severe test of three-year-olds than switchback Epsom.

Always in the end Derby Day has come back to Epsom Downs for it is only in these special surroundings that the occasion has been able to blossom. This is the place where the romance has remained, and that atmosphere that writers have attempted to reproduce in Victorian melodrama and musical comedy, sometimes with real horses on stage. The Derby has provided a climax for countless films. Perhaps because it is a childhood memory of my own, I would have thought that no filmed picture of the Derby scene has been more vivid than that which formed the high point of the first Technicolor picture made in England, *Wings of the Morning,* when just before the start of the race all the gypsies attending the occasion process down the course in order to prove that their queen is alive and that her horse is eligible to run in the race. It wins, of course. All quite preposterous; but just conceivable because it happened on that magic occasion, Derby Day.

Is the magic still there? Not so much today. Now there are far more roads to the course on which the racegoers may travel, but the various routes are still jammed with cars. As late as 1939 when the King and Queen used to drive to Epsom on the morning of the race, the crowds lined Clapham Common and other vantage points to cheer the high old royal Daimler as it made its stately progress. Now there is no acknowledgement of the royal presence until the Queen actually arrives at the course. While the Hill still has its fair and its touts, there is not the same feeling of carnival, and no one could call it a saturnalia. To a people with regular bank holidays and guaranteed annual leave, there cannot be the same relish in the stolen unofficial joys of Derby Day.

Who can count that myriad crowd? They made their guesses in Victorian times, and they do today. Sometimes they said that a quarter of a million people turned up, sometimes hundreds of thousands. It is probably still nearer the higher figure even though the television cameras can give a better picture of the race than that any occupant of the Hill can ever hope for. But, and this is the point, while television can show the race in every splendid detail, it cannot project the presence or the excitement of what is, after all, the population of a fair-size town who are all concentrating on one wonderful moment.

Perhaps today's is not a scene that Frith would recognise. There are no acrobats in spangles and the agricultural worker of today is far too fly to be conned out of his money by the shell game. The press of cars lacks the elegance of carriages and there is so much uniformity in the dress of Duke and dustman that it would not be easy to tell them apart. Few women today bet in gloves. I doubt if there are many lobster claws thrown about these days and the ground will be littered with more tins of beer than champagne bottles.

Frith's picture was exhibited in 1858. Let us imagine that it represents the 1857 Derby, and looking at the records we see that that year the filly Blink Bonny won the Derby and two days later turned out again and won the Oaks. A hundred years later Crepello was the winner. It is interesting to me that, in a world in which so many things have speeded up so much, there is only ten seconds difference between the time these horses took to cover the mile and a half. Indeed, Blink Bonny's time would have been good enough to win a number of recent Derbys. Now there are no false starts; the photofinish camera decides the result without question and the tracking cars provide a permanent record of any skulduggery among the jockeys on the course. The money that changes hands is much bigger; the stud fees mount ever higher, but the basics have not changed—in essence Derby Day remains essentially the same. The bell still rings, and for countless thousands there is no more magic moment than the almost whispered words that echo round the Downs: 'They're off'. In two and a half minutes the race will be over, but Derby Day will never be done.

The Derby Sweepstake, 1791, by I. N. Sartorius from a hand-coloured engraving in the Epsom Library. Photo John Bethell

The Road to Epsom, 1812, by T. Rowlandson. (Victoria & Albert Museum).

Return from the Derby, Clapham Common, 1862, by J. F. Herring.
Photo John Bethell

EPSOM RACES on the Derby Day, 1841, by T. Allom, from a hand-coloured engraving

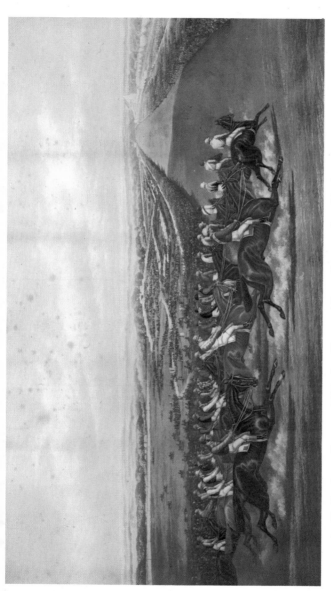

Tattenham Corner, 1820, by Henry Alken from a hand-coloured engraving in the Epsom Library. Photo John Bethell

The Effects of a Windy Day, 1820, Artist unknown.
From an aquatint in the Epsom Library. Photo John Bethell

Le Derby d'Epsom from a painting by **Jean Géricault** *c.* 1821 in The Louvre.
Photo **Bulloz**

Epsom, The Betting Post, 1830, by J. Pollard from an engraving in The British Museum.
Photo J. R. Freeman & Co

Epsom, Saddling in the Warren, c. 1830 by J. Pollard from an engraving in the British Museum.

Epsom, Preparing to Start, 1830, by J. Pollard from an engraving in the British Museum.
Photo J. R. Freeman & Co

The Winner of the Derby, 1836, by J. Pollard from an engraving in the British Museum.

The Start for the Memorable Derby of 1844, by J. F. Herring from a contemporary engraving.
(Messrs Fores)

Derby Day, 1858, from a painting by W. P. Frith in the Tate Gallery.
Photo A. C. Cooper Ltd